Old World Monkeys

Published by Wildlife Education, Ltd.
9820 Willow Creek Road, Suite 300, San Diego, California 92131

ISBN 0-937934-92-5

Old World Monkeys

Series Created by
John Bonnett Wexo

Written by
Ann Elwood

Zoological Consultant
Charles R. Schroeder, D.V.M.
Director Emeritus
San Diego Zoo and San Diego Wild Animal Park

Scientific Consultant
Donald Lindburg, Ph.D.
Behaviorist
Zoological Society of San Diego

Zoobooks

Art Credits

Illustrations by Richard Orr
Inside Front Cover: Walter Stuart

Photographic Credits

Front Cover: George H. Harrison *(Grant Heilman)*

Pages Six and Seven: Erwin and Peggy Bauer *(Bruce Coleman, Inc.)*

Page Ten: Jany Sauvanet *(Photo Researchers)*

Page Eleven: Mickey Gibson *(Animals Animals)*

Page Twelve: Philip A. Savoie *(Bruce Coleman, Inc.)*

Page Thirteen: Gerry Ellis *(Ellis Wildlife)*

Pages Fourteen and Fifteen: Gerry Ellis *(Ellis Wildlife)*

Page Sixteen: Steven C. Kaufman *(Peter Arnold)*

Page Seventeen: **Middle Right**: Rod Williams *(Bruce Coleman, Ltd.)*; **Lower Right**, Anthony Bannister *(NHPA)*

Page Eighteen: Richard K. LaVal *(Animals Animals)*

Page Nineteen: **Upper Right**: A.J. Deane *(Bruce Coleman, Ltd.)*; **Middle Left**, Belinda Wright *(DRK Photo)*

Pages Twenty and Twenty-one: Gary Milburn *(Tom Stack and Associates)*

Page Twenty-two: **Upper Left**: C.B. Frith *(Bruce Coleman, Ltd.)*

Mask Series: Gordon Menzie

Page Twenty-three: Gordon Menzie

Our Thanks To: Thelma Rowell and Janis Chism *(Dept. of Integrative Biology, UC Berkeley)*; Linda Coates, Valerie Hare, Wendy Perkins *(San Diego Zoo Library)*; Casey and Lizzie Elwood; Geoffrey Lowman; and Joe Selig

Cover Photo: Mandrill

Contents

Monkeys seem to be a lot like us. They are curious. They show their feelings on their faces. And they have two arms and two legs, five fingers and five toes, and human-looking eyes and ears. This is not too surprising, because like us and our cousins the apes, monkeys are primates, whose ancestors had bodies that were adapted to life in the trees. Even though some monkeys live mostly on the ground, their eyes, hands, feet, and brains show their heritage.

Scientists divide monkeys into two groups— *Old World monkeys* and *New World monkeys*. Old World monkeys live in Africa and Asia, mainly in rain forests and in woodland-grassland regions (see map below). They are different in several ways from New World monkeys, which live in Central and South America. For example, their nostrils are smaller and closer together, and some of them have callouses on their back ends like built-in seat cushions. Many New World monkeys have *prehensile* (pre-HEN-suhl) tails, tails that can grasp objects in much the same way that a hand can. But Old World monkeys do not have prehensile tails.

On the surface, Old World monkeys *look* very different from each other. Some have faces that look like masks, others are bearded, and still others have crests on their heads. Some, like the monkey on the cover of this book, have amazingly colorful faces. Colobus monkeys have beautiful, furry tails, but some monkeys have tails that are so small you can barely see them. The biggest Old World monkeys are the drill and the mandrill, which can weigh up to 110 pounds (50 kilograms) each. The smallest is the talapoin, which weighs as little as 1½ pounds (680 grams).

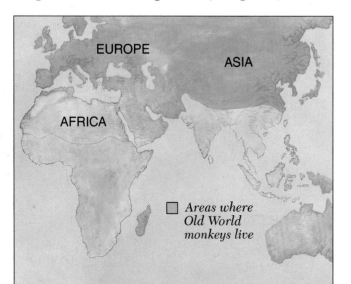

EUROPE

ASIA

AFRICA

☐ *Areas where Old World monkeys live*

Young yellow baboon

The **82 species of Old World monkeys** come in a variety of shapes, sizes, and colors. In general, Old World monkeys can be divided into two subfamilies—the *cercopithecines* (sir-cuh-PITH-uh-ceens) and the *colobines* (COLL-uh-beans). The cercopithecines eat fruit and many other types of food, and they have big cheek pouches in which to carry it. The colobines are usually more slender, and they lack cheek pouches. Mainly leaf eaters, they have highly specialized stomachs to help them break down and digest their food.

ZANZIBAR RED COLOBUS
Colobus badius kirkii
(Colobine)

BLACK-AND-WHITE COLOBUS
Colobus guereza
(Colobine)

TALAPOIN
Miopithecus talapoin
(Cercopithecine)

DE BRAZZA'S MONKEY
Cercopithecus neglectus
(Cercopithecine)

MANDRILL
Papio sphinx
(Cercopithecine)

NILGIRI LANGUR
Presbytis johni
(Colobine)

SOOTY MANGABEY
Cercocebus torquatus
(Cercopithecine)

DIANA MONKEY
Cercopithecus diana
(Cercopithecine)

HAMADRYAS BABOON
Papio hamadryas
(Cercopithecine)

GOLDEN SNUB-NOSED MONKEY
Rhinopithecus roxellana
(Colobine)

PROBOSCIS MONKEY
Nasalis larvatus
(Colobine)

HANUMAN LANGUR
Presbytis entellus
(Colobine)

DOUC LANGUR
Pygathrix nemaeus
(Colobine)

PIG-TAILED MACAQUE
Macaca nemestrina
(Cercopithecine)

9

DE BRAZZA'S MONKEY

The bodies of all monkeys evolved for life in the trees. All monkeys have hands and feet that can grasp onto branches. And their eyes, like ours, are made for seeing things in three dimensions. This is especially important for tree dwellers, which need to judge distances from branch to branch and from branch to ground.

The ways in which monkeys' bodies differ from species to species has a lot to do with where they live and what they eat. For example, tree-dwelling monkeys have limber bodies that are perfect for leaping between branches. And ground-dwelling monkeys have shorter, more robust bodies built for surviving on the ground.

Monkeys that live in trees use their tails to balance and steer themselves, and to help them brake when they leap from branch to branch.

RED HOWLER MONKEY

Monkeys have strong arm and leg muscles. Tree-dwelling monkeys have especially strong hind legs for leaping across branches. And ground-dwelling monkeys have long front limbs and heavy shoulder muscles for walking on all fours.

Only New World monkeys, like this red howler monkey, have prehensile tails. They use these strong, muscular tails to grasp branches. Having a prehensile tail is almost like having an extra hand!

The cercopithecines have special pouches in their cheeks for carrying their food. They stuff the pouches with food, then move to a safe place to eat it. This leaves their hands and feet free for running and climbing. A monkey can hold as much food in its cheeks as it can in its stomach!

Like humans, monkeys have fingernails, sensitive fingertips, and individual fingerprints

GRAY-CHEEKED MAGABEY

All monkeys have hands that can hook around a tree branch. This so-called *power grip* is what keeps them from falling when they are up in the trees. It is also what enables them to grab leaves off of branches. Some monkeys, like the colobus at left, have shorter thumbs than others— but they can still hang on.

Many primates, including humans and some monkeys, can touch their fingers with their long, flexible thumbs. Because of this ability, a monkey can pinch a piece of grass between its thumb and fingers and pluck it. Monkeys can pick up small objects.

All monkeys have big eye sockets, and their eyes are set in the *front* of their heads. Monkeys also have *binocular vision*— this enables them to look at an object with both eyes at once. It also gives them the ability to see things in depth.

A monkey has 32 teeth —the same number that you have. Colobines have teeth that are good for eating leaves. Cercopithecines have teeth that are made to eat almost anything.

A monkey's bones are light and flexible enough for leaping and traveling through the trees. Sitting upright in a tree, a monkey can grab food with one hand while holding onto a branch with the other. And it can grip a second branch with its feet while using its tail as a balancer.

Monkey babies get lots of love and attention. When a baby is born, members of the troop are quick to come and see it. Monkey mothers usually have only one baby at a time. The baby's eyes are open at birth, and it has fur. Though quite helpless in most other ways, it is born with the ability to cling to its mother with its hands and feet. Being able to cling is very useful for a baby whose mother uses her hands and feet to get around in the trees.

Monkey children have long childhoods — sometimes lasting up to three years. When they are very young, the babies stay close to their mothers. Then, as they grow older, they begin to play with other young monkeys. They chase each other, pull each other's tails, and play follow-the-leader. By playing together, young monkeys learn how to live in a group. And they develop physical skills that are important for life on the ground and in the trees.

When it is very young, a monkey baby rides on the underside of its mother's body. It clings tightly to her fur and goes almost everywhere she goes.

PROBOSCIS MONKEYS

Some monkey babies look very different from their parents. This proboscis (pro-BAH-suss) baby, for instance, has a tiny turned-up nose, while its father has a big hanging nose. Proboscis babies also have blue faces. Scientists are not quite sure why this is. Perhaps it is to help the adults recognize the babies as "special."

INDIAN LANGURS

A monkey mother may grab her youngster by the tail to keep it from straying too far and getting into trouble. A young monkey could get hurt by playing too rough with an older youngster. Or, worse, it could be "kidnapped" by another female who wants a baby of her own.

Monkeys groom each other by running their fingers through each other's fur and picking out bits of dirt, insects, and dry skin. This older child is grooming its parent. In this way, monkeys show their affection for each other. They also help keep each other's fur clean and free from parasites.

When they can, monkey mothers will fight to protect their babies from danger. This mother patas (PAT-us) monkey is making it very clear to the jackal to stay away from her baby or else! Other adult monkeys besides the mother will also care for and protect babies.

Monkeys are among the most social of all animals. They enjoy each other's company, and spend a great deal of time in close contact with one another. These olive baboons are wrestling playfully in the grass.

onkeys behave in ways that help them to survive. Because they lack horns, scales, poisons, fighting ability, and other forms of self-defense, they rely mostly on their wits to stay out of danger. As a group, monkeys learn quickly and adapt easily to new situations. And for this reason, they are very successful animals.

Monkeys are also very social animals. They live together in groups called *troops*. But some monkeys live in larger troops than others. Gelada (juh-LAH-duh) monkeys, for instance, like the ones shown on these pages, sometimes band together in huge troops of several hundred animals. By sticking close together, monkeys have a better chance of detecting predators such as snakes, lions, hyenas, cheetahs, leopards, people, and other primates.

When two males are quarreling, the other monkeys in the troop stay out of their way.

JAPANESE MACAQUES (SNOW MONKEYS)

GELADA MONKEYS

Some macaque monkeys, like these snow monkeys of Japan, climb into hot springs to stay warm in winter. They sit in the water up to their necks until they get hungry. Then they dash out for a bite to eat. Thick hair on their heads helps to protect their ears from the cold.

These gelada males are "flipping their lips" at each other as a warning that they are ready to fight. Notice how their upper lips are curled back so they can show each other their big canine teeth. Sometimes the "lip flip" alone is enough to prevent a fight, causing one of the monkeys to give up and withdraw.

16

Monkeys sometimes join up with other animals for better protection against predators. They do not hear or smell as well as most grazing animals. But they do see better. Here baboons and gazelles herd together. If the baboons don't see a predator, the gazelles will probably hear or smell it. Either way, when one animal calls out an alarm all the others are warned of danger.

DOUC LANGUR

Colobine monkeys are vegetarians. Most of them, like this douc langur (DUKE LANG-uhr), eat leaves and other plant parts as their main diet. However, they also like fruits, flowers, seeds, and insects.

BABOON

Cercopithecines eat a variety of foods, including plants. They have been known to dine on fruit, flowers, leaves, bark, grass, bulbs, insects, crabs, bird eggs, and lizards. Occasionally baboons, like the one at right, even eat meat.

Some cultures worship monkeys, and others treat them badly. But no matter what the human attitude is, many monkeys are in danger because their habitat is shrinking.

Cultures that worship monkeys protect them from harm. But in other cultures, monkeys are hunted for their fur and for meat. They are killed because people use the stones in their stomachs as medicine. Monkeys are also destroyed by farmers who catch them raiding their crops.

Still, the biggest danger to monkeys is loss of habitat. And many species, especially those that live in rain forests, are endangered because of this. Special land has been set aside for monkeys in many parts of Asia and Africa. But this is only the first step toward saving them.

CAPPED LANGUR
Presbytis pileata

DIANA MONKEY
Cercopithecus diana

LION-TAILED MACAQUE
Macaca silenus

SOOTY MANGABEY
Cercocebus torquatus

FRANCOIS' LANGUR
Presbytis francoisi

Every day, forests that provide homes for monkeys are being chopped down. They are being cleared to provide wood, to make space for homes, to create grasslands for cattle grazing, or to plant rice or corn. But there are ways that monkey habitats could be saved. For instance, loggers could cut down a few trees and leave the rest so that the forest would remain—then monkeys would still have a place to live.

All of the monkey species in this tree are in danger of losing their habitats. Unless something is done to save them, these species could disappear from the earth completely.

L'HOEST'S MONKEY
Cercopithecus l'hoesti

PROBOSCIS MONKEY
Nasalis larvatus

PIG-TAILED LANGUR
Simias concolor

Some religious people in India consider monkeys to be sacred. In fact, until recently, they let them live on the grounds of their temples, pick fruit from their gardens, and even eat from their tables. But today, more and more people in India consider the monkeys to be pests. And because they raid their crops, farmers even kill them sometimes.

HANUMAN LANGURS

RUST-RED COLOBUS
Colobus badius

RHESUS MACAQUE

Around the turn of the century, millions of monkeys were killed for their hides to make monkey fur coats. Monkey fur is still being sold to tourists today—for rugs as well as for coats. But monkey fur does *not* belong on people's backs or on the floor—it belongs on monkeys!

Some forest-dwelling monkeys have lost a large part of their habitat to farmers. Because wild food is scarce, they have learned to raid farmers' crops. And they are very clever at doing this. They wait until there is a rainstorm or until people are napping. Then they rush in and steal the food. Some monkeys will even chase workers off the field so that they can eat the vegetables growing in it.

VERVETS

19

Golden snub-nosed monkeys, shown in this picture, live in the cold mountains of western China. These monkeys spend much of their time hugging each other, probably to stay warm.

MONKEYS
ACTIVITIES

Use what you have learned about Old World monkeys to complete the fun activities on these two pages.

Hole to let in light

Peep-hole

Cutaway to show inside (do not cut).

Monkey Masks

Make several monkey masks to show different monkey faces. Then you and your friends can wear the masks while acting out monkey behaviors you have read about in this book. You will need: *paper plates, colored construction paper, glue, and scissors.*

Study the pictures in this book. Notice the expressions that different monkeys make. Pay close attention to the monkeys' mouths, which show the most expression.

1. Choose one monkey face for each mask you wish to make. Quickly sketch the shapes of each monkey's eyes, nose, mouth, head, and ears on a piece of scratch paper.

Monkey Around With Some Facts

Unscramble the capital letters to review some facts about monkeys.

2. Choose the colors of construction paper that you will use for each mask. Cut out the construction paper to match the shapes of the monkeys' features that you observed and sketched.

3. For each mask, glue the cut out construction paper onto a paper plate. Poke and then carefully cut eye holes in the mask. *Warning: Do not wear the mask while cutting the eye holes.* Tie string to each mask to help hold it in place when you wear it.

2.

All monkeys can wrap their hands around a tree branch to keep from LALIGNF.

2. Falling

3.

Some monkeys are LAICOS animals that live in large groups.

3. Social

5.

Because they have big RANSIB, monkeys can learn and adapt to new situations.

5. Brains

1.

6.

22

Monkey Diorama

You can create an environment for your pipe cleaner monkeys to live in when they are not hanging around your house. Use a cardboard box with a lid.

1. Cut a peephole in one end of your box for looking at the diorama. Also cut a hole in the top of the box to let light in.

2. Think about the kind of environment you want your monkeys to live in. Will it be a tropical forest? Will it be a woodland? A grassland? Or will it have a hot spring like those in Japan? Will the environment be safe for the monkeys? Or will you include some kind of danger, such as trees being cut down or a predator that might attack them?

3. Collect the things you will need to make the environment the way you want it. You might use clay, paint, real or plastic plants, rocks, paper, cloth, ribbons, cotton balls, and other found objects. Use paste, staples, and bits of clay to attach all the parts inside the box.

4. When you are finished, look through the peephole. Is everything where you want it to be? Did you decorate the lid of the box? Are there things for your monkeys to hang from? When you like the way your box looks, let your monkeys enjoy their new home.

Read More About Monkeys

Picture Library Monkeys and Apes by N. S. Barrett. New York: Franklin Watts, 1988.

Have you ever wondered about the differences between apes, monkeys, and people? Would you like to know what different expressions on monkeys' faces mean? Do you know what an aye-aye looks like? What is growing up like for a young monkey? This colorfully photographed book holds the answers to these and other interesting questions about monkeys.

Monkeys: The Japanese Macaques by Cynthia Overbeck. Photographs by Osamu Nishikawa. Minneapolis: Lerner Publications, 1981.

See Japanese macaques in their natural surroundings, which range from sunny beaches to snow-covered mountains. Watch young macaques at play and learning old habits, as well as finding ways to improve the way they live in their environment.

Some monkeys have long, flexible HUMBST.

1. Thumbs

Monkeys MOGRO a baby by running their fingers through its fur.

4. Groom

4.

Monkey Fruit Salad

Imagine that a troop of monkeys is coming to your home for lunch. What should you serve them? Try this fruit salad filled with foods that monkeys love to eat. *(Ask an adult to help you cut the fruit.)* Then invite your friends over for lunch and to try some of the activities on these pages.

Cut into bite-sized pieces:

    1 apple, 1 banana, 1 orange
    Other fruit in season

Grate:

    1 carrot

Remove the shells from:

    ⅔ cup (185 ml) sunflower seeds
    1 cup (275 ml) peanuts

Mix together all the ingredients. If you like, add 1 cup (240 ml) yogurt.

Pipe Cleaner Monkey

Create interesting sculptures of monkeys. All you need is some pipe cleaners and your imagination.

1. Twist the ends of two pipe cleaners together. Bend the pair into this shape to make the legs. Curl the ends to make hooked feet.

2. Use two more pipe cleaners to make the arms. Then curl the ends of the arms to make hooked hands.

3. Now twist the ends of two more pipe cleaners together. Spread these in the middle to make the body of the monkey.

4. Attach the arms at the top of the body and the legs at the bottom.

5. Cut a pipe cleaner in half with scissors. Curl it up to make a head like the one shown. Attach the head to the body. Then add a tail.

Index